# IPAD MINI 6 USER GUIDE

## A Complete Step By Step Manual For Beginners and Seniors On How To Navigate Through The New 8.3" iPad Mini 6th Generation With Tips & Tricks For iPadOS

BY

TONY D. FOGG

# Copyright © 2021 TONY D. FOGG

**Table of Contents**

# INTRODUCTION

Apple unveiled the sixth -generation iPad mini in September 2021, two and a half years after the release of the foregoing model, with a larger display, no Home button, the A15 Bionic chip, USB-C port, and support for the 2nd Generation Apple Pencil.

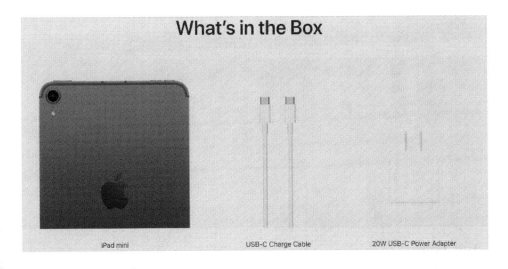

# FEATURES OF IPAD MINI 6

## Design

With the release of the 6th generation iPad mini, Apple has completely redesigned its design and it now looks like the iPad Air.

The 6th gen iPad mini has an 8.3-inch display, which is bigger than the 7.9-inch iPad mini 5 due to less bezel around the screen.

Like the iPad Air, the 6ᵗʰ gen iPad mini has a flat body, with rounded edges that wrap around the screen. The iPad mini has a small bezel around its screen.

The iPad mini is 195.4mm long, 134.8mm wide & 6.3mm thick. The device does not have headphone jack.

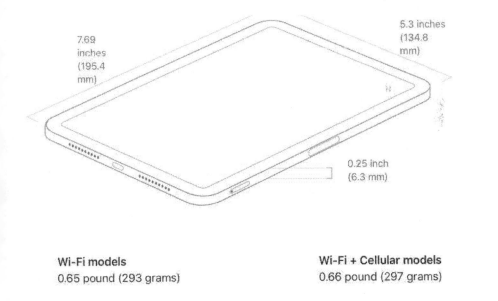

At the top of the device, you would find the volume buttons. The volume button is at the top to create space for a magnetic connector on the side that is utilized to charge the 2nd-gen Apple Pencil.

The device is available in Starlight, Purple, Pink, & Space Gray.

## Touch ID

The Touch ID button is at the top of the device and requires you to put your finger to unlock the device.

You can use the Touch ID to access applications, buy with Apple Pay, etc.

Long pressing the Touch ID power button would summon Siri.

# Display

The device has an 8.3-inch laminated screen with a resolution of 2266 by 1488 at 326pixels per inch. The 6<sup>th</sup> gen iPad mini is compatible with wide colour for clear, true-to-life colours, and comes with support for True Tone.

# Apple pencil

The previous-gen iPad mini supported the 1<sup>st</sup> gen Apple Pencil, while the iPad mini 6 is compatible with the 2<sup>nd</sup> generation Apple Pencil.

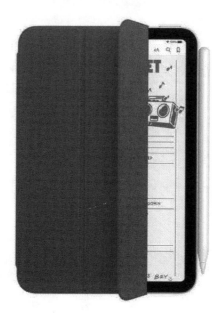

The magnetic strip beside the device lets the 2nd gen Apple Pencil connect to the iPad & charge.

## A15 Bionic chip

The Mini iPad has a 6-core A15 chip. The chip allows the iPad mini 6 to offer about 40% faster single-core performance, 70% faster multi-core performance, and 80% faster graphics than the previous-gen iPad mini A12 chip.

## RAM

The iPad mini 6 has 4GB of RAM.

## Storage Space

The main iPad mini has 64 GB of storage and a 256 GB upgrade is available.

## Back camera

The device has $f$ / 1.8 a 12-megapixel rear camera with a digital zoom of about 5x, a quad-LED True Tone flash, and a 5-component lens.

4K video formats are supported at 24, 25, 30, or 60 frames per second, as well as slo-mo videos at 120 or 240 frames per second.

## Front Camera & Center Stage

There is also a front camera with an f / 2.4 driver and a 122-degree view field, which is compatible with Center Stage. The Center Stage feature ensures you remain in focus and completely framed when making a FaceTime video call.

## Battery life

The device has a 19.3-watt battery. According to Apple, the battery lasts about 10 hours while surfing the Internet or watching videos, and the cellular models last about 9 hours when surfing the Internet on a cellular connection.

## 5G

The 6th gen iPad mini has a 5G chip that lets it connect to a 5G network, but unlike the 5G iPhones for the United States, it is not compatible with the fastest mmWave 5G network.

# SETUP YOUR IPAD

**1** Hold down the power button till the Apple logo is displayed on your screen. "Hello" would be displayed in many languages.

Top button

When prompted, select your language. Then click on your region or country. This would affect how the information would look on your iPad

**2** If you have another device, it can be used to setup the new device with the Quick Start feature. Bring both devices close to each other, and adhere to the directives on your display.

If you do not have another device, touch the **Setup Manually** button to continue.

3 You need to connect to a WiFi network, mobile network, or iTunes to enable and continue the setup of your device.

Click on the Wi-Fi network you want to utilize or choose another option.

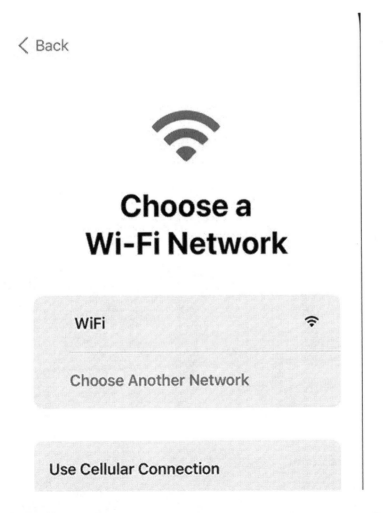

**4** The next step is to setup Touch ID. With the Touch ID feature, your fingerprint can be used to open your iPad and buy things online. Touch **Continue** and adhere to the directives on your display or touch **Setup Later in Settings**.

Then, generate a 6- digit code to protect your data. You need a password to use features Touch ID & Apple Pay. You can touch **Passcode Options** for more password options

**5** If you have backed up your previous device with iCloud or PC or Android device, you can restore data or move your info from your old device to your iPad.

If you do not have a backup or other device, choose **Do not transfer applications and data**.

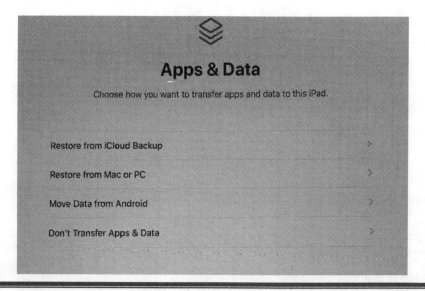

**6** Enter your Apple ID & password, or touch "Forgot passcode or do you have an Apple ID?" Then, you can reset your Apple ID or password, create an Apple ID, or create it later. If you have multiple Apple IDs, touch **Use different Apple IDs on iCloud and iTunes?**

After signing in with your Apple ID, you may be asked for a verification code from your previous device.

< Back                                    Next

## Apple ID

Sign in with your Apple ID to use iCloud, the
App Store, and other Apple services.

| | |
|---|---|
| Apple ID | j.appleseed@icloud.com |
| Password | Required |

Forgot password or don't have an Apple ID?

Your Apple ID information is used to enable Apple services when
you sign in, including iCloud Backup which automatically backs up
the data on your device in case you need to replace or restore it.
Your device serial number may be used to check eligibility for
service offers. See how your data is managed...

Use different Apple IDs for iCloud & other

7 On the next displays, you can choose to share your data with application developers & permit iOS to automatically update.

8 Next, you will be told to setup or activate features & services, such as Siri. You might be told to say a few sentences so that Siri will recognize your voice.

If you are logged in with your Apple ID, adhere to the directives to setup Apple Pay & iCloud Keychain.

9 The Screen Time feature provides insight into the time you and your child spend using your device. It also lets you set time limits for daily application usage. After setting up Screen Time, you can activate True Tone, and utilize Display Zoom to adjust the icons & text size on the Home screen.

10 Click on the **Get Start** button to start making use of your iPad.

# IPAD BASIC GESTURES

Control your device & the applications in it with a few gestures.

**Tap:** Touch your screen with a finger

**Touch & hold, Hold down, or Long press**: Touch & hold the items in an application to view contents & perform quick actions. Press & hold an application icon on your Home screen to launch the **quick action menu**.

**Swipe:** Quickly move one finger on your display.

↑

**Scroll:** move a finger across your display without raising your finger.

---

**Zoom:** put two of your fingers on your display close to each other. Spread them out to zoom in, or bring them close to each other to zoom out.

When viewing a photo or when on a webpage you can zoom in by double-tapping your screen, double-tap once more to zoom out.

**Go Home:** swipe up from the lower part of your screen, to return to your Home screen.

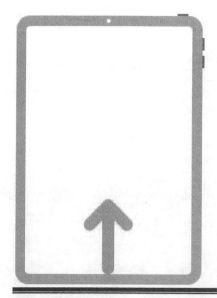

**Open the Control center:** Swipe down from the upper right part of your display to reveal the Control Centre; hold down any control to display more options.

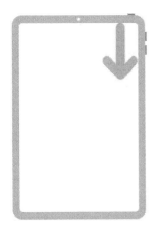

**Open the application Switcher:** Swipe up from the lower part of your display, stop at the middle of your display, and then raise your finger. Swipe right to view other open applications and then touch the application you want to utilize.

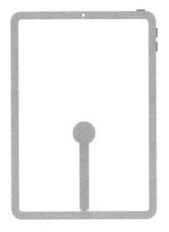

**Open the Dock in an application**: Swipe up from the lower part of your display and stop to show the Dock.

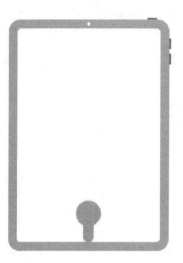

**Ask Siri:** Hold down the top button while stating your request. Then release the button when you are done

**Utilize Accessibility Shortcut:** Press the top button three times.

**Switch off:** long press the top & any of the volume button simultaneously till the slider appears, and then move the slide to power off. Or, enter the Setting application> General> ShutDown.

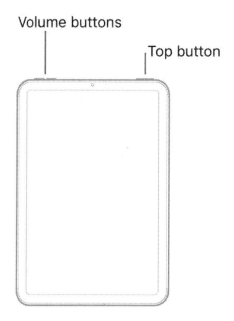

Volume buttons

Top button

**Force restart:** Press & leave the volume up button, press & leave the volume down button, then hold down the top button till the Apple icon appears.

**Capture the screen:** Press & release the top & any of the volume buttons simultaneously.

# IPAD ESSENTIALS

## Wake up your iPad

The display of your iPad turns off to save power, locks for safety, and sleeps when you are not making use of it. You can wake up your device when you want to use it.

To wake your device, do any of the below:

- Press the top button.

Top button

- Touch the display.

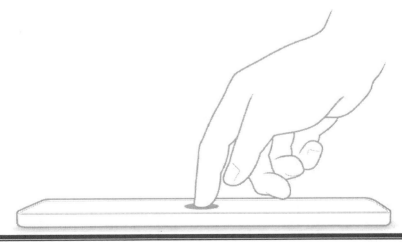

---

# Unlock your device

If you activate Touch ID while setting up your device, you can unlock your device by pressing the top button with the finger you registered on Touch ID

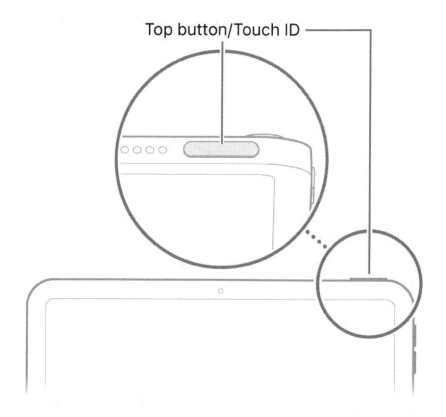

Top button/Touch ID

Press the button again to lock your device. If you do not touch the screen for a minute, the iPad automatically locks.

**Unlock your device with a password**

If you created a passcode while setting up your device, you can unlock your device by swiping up from the lower part of your lock screen, then enter your password

## Insert a SIM card

You can insert an Apple SIM card or a SIM card provided by a carrier.

- Put the SIM ejecting tool into the small hole of the SIM plate, and push it towards the device to bring out the tray.

- Take the tray out of the iPad.
- Put your SIM in the tray.

- Put the tray in the iPad.
- If you have already set a PIN on the SIM, enter the PIN correctly when asked to.

## Connect your iPad to Wi-Fi

- Enter the Settings application> Wi-Fi, and activate Wi-Fi.
- Click on one of the below:
  - ➤ Network: Enter a password if necessary.
  - ➤ Others: Join a secret network. Enter the name, security type, and password of the secret network.

When the Wi-Fi icon 📶 appears at the upper part of your display, the iPad is connected to the Wi-Fi network.

## Connect your iPad to a mobile network (Wi-Fi + Cellular model)

The iPad automatically connects to the carrier's cellular system when there is no Wi-Fi network. If the iPad is not connected, check the following:

- Ensure your SIM card is open & activated.

- Enter the Settings application> Cellular data.
- Check that the cellular data is enabled.

## App Library

The Application library displays the application on your device arranged into categories, which include information & reading, productivity & finance, and creativity.

To find & launch an application in the Application Library

- Tap the Application Library button  on the Dock.

Go to App Library

- Touch the search box at the upper part of your display, then enter the name of the application you want. Otherwise, scroll through the alphabetical list.
- Touch an application to launch it.

## Hide & display the home screen pages

Since you can see all the applications in the application library, you may not need many Home screen pages. You can hide some of the home screen pages

- Hold down the Home screen till the applications start jiggling.
- Touch the dots at the lower part of your display.

The home screen is displayed with thumbnails of your pages, along with check marks under them.

- To hide pages, remove the checkmark by tapping on it. Touch to add checkmarks to display the pages you have hidden.
- After adding or removing the pages, touch the Home screen background two times.

## Dictate on iPad

With the Dictation feature on your iPad mini, you can dictate text wherever you can type it.

### Activating dictation

- Enter the Setting application> General> Keyboard.

- Activate Enable Dictation.

**To dictate text**

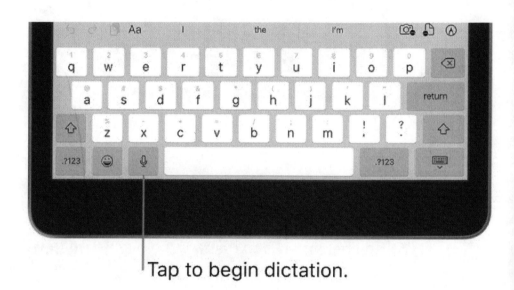

Tap to begin dictation.

- Touch the Dict key 🎤 on the on-screen keyboard, and start talking.

  If you can't find the Dictate button 🎤, ensure Dictation is Enabled in the Settings application> General> Keyboards.

- When you are done, press the Keypad ⌨.

To use the dictation feature, tap on the entry point where you want to insert text, press the Dictate key 🎤 & speak.

**To add punctuation, follow the directives below:**

Say a punctuation mark while dictating.

For instance, "Hello Sam Comma the test result has been sent to your e-mail Full-Stop" would become "Hello Sam, the test result has been sent to your e-mail."

## Select & Edit text

In applications on your device, you can utilize the keyboard on your screen to select & edit text in the text field.

1. To highlight text, do any of the below:
   - ➢ Highlight a word: tap on the word two times with a finger.
   - ➢ Highlight a paragraph: three taps with a finger.
   - ➢ Highlight a sentence: double-tap & hold the first word in the sentence then drag it to the last word.
2. Once you have selected the text you want to edit, you can write or click on the option to view the editing options:

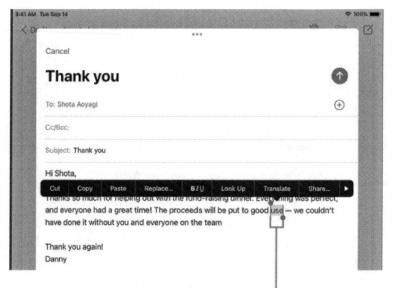

Tap the selected text
to see options.

> Cut.

> Copy.

> Paste.

> Replace: See the suggested replacement text or allow Siri to suggest a different text.

> B / I / U: format the highlighted text.

> ▶ See other options.

## Text replacement

Create a text replacement that can be used to replace words or phrases by typing just a few letters. For instance, Enter **omw** to insert **on my way**.

## To create text substitutions

1.  Do any of the below:
    ➢ With the on-screen keyboard: Press & hold the Emoji button☺, or Switch keypad button⊕, touch Keyboard settings, and touch Text Replacement.
    ➢ With an external keyboard: Enter the Settings application> General> Keyboard, then touch Text Replacement.
2.  Touch the Add button✛ on the upper right corner of your display.
3.  Write a short sentence in the sentence box & the text shortcut you plan on using in the shortcut box.

## Add or remove a keyboard

- Enter the Setting application, touch General, and touch Keyboards.
- Touch the keyboard, then do any of the below:

---

- ➢ Add keyboard: Touch **Add a new keyboard** and then select a keyboard from the catalog.
- ➢ Delete keyboard: Touch the edit button, click the erase button  beside the Keyboard you plan on erasing, touch the Delete button, and then touch Done.

## Multitask using picture in picture

With the Picture-in-Picture feature, you can make a FaceTime call or watch a movie while using other applications.

While watching a movie, touch the reduce size button .

The video window would scale down to one part of your display so that you can see your home screen and use other applications. While the video or FaceTime window is still showing, you can do any of the below:

- Change the video window size: pinch open on the window to increase the size or pinch close to reduce it.
- Display or conceal Controls: Touch the video window.
- Change the location of the window on your display: drag the window to another part of your display.
- Hide the window by dragging it to the right or left edge of your display.
- Close window: Click the Close button .
- Back to the full video screen: Touch the image button in the window.

# Access features from your lock screen

Even when your device is locked, you can quickly access the functions and information you need on the Lock screen.

- Launch the camera: swipe to the left.
- Launch the Controls centre: Swipe down from the upper right corner of your display
- See previous message: swipe up from the middle of your display.

- To view widgets: swipe right.
- To take notes or draw: Use the Apple Pencil to swipe diagonally from the bottom-right edge of your display. Anything created is stored in Notes.

## Display notifications preview on the Lock Screen

- Enter the settings application, touch Notifications.
- Touch Show previews, then click on Always.

## Perform quick actions

- In the photo application, press & hold a picture to preview and view the list of options.
- In the Mail application, long press a message in the mail box to get the message preview, and see an Options list.
- On the Home screen, long press an application icon to launch a quick actions menu. If the icons start jiggling, touch Done at the upper right part of your display, and try again.

- Launch the Control Centre, and hold down an item, such as Camera or brightness Control, to find more options.
- On the lock screen, hold down a notification to reply to it.
- When you type, long-press the spacebar with a finger to turn the keyboard into a track pad.

## Search with iPad

1. Swipe down from the centre of the Home or Lock screen.

2. Touch the search box, and type whatever you want.

3. Do any of the below:

   ➢ Conceal the keyboard and view more results on your display: Press the search key.

   ➢ Launch a suggested application: Touch it.

   ➢ Find out more about a certain search result: Touch it, and touch one of the results to open it.

   ➢ Begin another search: Touch the Clear text button ⊗ in the search box.

# Use AirDrop to send items to nearby devices

With AirDrop, you can wirelessly transfer your pictures, sites, locations, etc. to devices that are close to you (iOS 7, iPadOS 13, OS X 10.10 or after required). AirDrop sends data via Wi -Fi & Bluetooth - both should be activated. The transfer is encrypted for security.

## Send items via AirDrop

- Open what you want to send, and touch Share, ⬆️, AirDrop, More Options••• or any other button that shows the share options of the application.

- Touch the AirDrop icon 📶 in the list of share options, then touch the nearby AirDrop user profile image.

If the individual is not showing as a close-by AirDrop user, tell them to open the Control Centre on their iPhone, iPad, or iPod touch and allow AirDrop receive items. To send to people making use of Macs, tell them to let themselves be found in AirDrop in the Finder.

**Let others send things to your iPad via AirDrop**

- Open the Controls centre, hold down the upper left panel of the controls, and then touch the AirDrop icon 📶.

- Touch Only Contacts or Everybody to select people you want to get things from.

# Take a screenshot on your device

- Press & release the top button and any of the volume buttons simultaneously.
- Touch the screenshot in the bottom left part, and then touch done.
- Select Save to Photos or Files, or delete the screenshot.

# Store a full-Page screen shot as a PDF

You can capture a fullpage, scrolling screen shot of a web page, doc, or e-mail that is longer than the screen length of your device, and store it as a PDF file.

- Press & release the top & any of the volume buttons simultaneously.
- Touch the screenshot in the bottom-left part of your display, then touch Full Page.
- Do any of the below:
  - ➢ Store the screen shot: Touch Done, Select Store PDF to Files, select a location and click the Save button.
  - ➢ Share screen shot: Touch the Share button, select a sharing option, enter other needed info, and send the file.

# Magnify objects close to your device

In the Magnifier application, you can utilize your device as a magnifying glass to magnify things around you.

---

## Activate the magnifier

Launch the Magnifier application in any of the ways below:

- Click the magnifier application icon  from the Home screen or the Application Library

- Open the Controls Centre, then press the Magnifier button 🔍.

  (If you can't find the Magnifier button 🔍, add it to the Control Center – by launching the Settings application> Controls Centre, then select Magnifier).

**To edit the image**

Do any of the below:

- Adjust the zoom level by dragging the zoom control slide to the right or left.
- View more controls by swiping the controls up.
- Change the brightness: touch the brightness button ☀️
- Change the contrast: Touch ◐.
- Use color filtering: click the Filter button ⬚.
- Add more light: Press the flashlight button 🔦 to turn on the light.

# Display the battery level in the status bar

Enter the Settings application> Battery, and activate Battery Percentage.

# Create a screen recording

You record your display & capture the sound as well.

- Enter the Settings application> Control Center, then touch the Add button beside Screen Recording.

- Open the controls centre, touch the record button, and then wait for three seconds before your device starts recording.

- To stop the recording, open the Controls Centre, touch or the red Status Bar at the upper part of your display, then touch the Stop button.

Go to the Photos application, then choose the screen recording.

# Set alarm on your iPad

In the Clock application, you can set an alarm that would play a ringing tone at a specified time.

- Click on Alarm, then touch the Add button
- Set the time, and select any of the options below:
  - ➢ Repeat: Select the days.

- label: Name the alarm something like "Water the crops".
- Sound: Select a ringing tone.
- Snooze: Give yourself 9 extra minutes.
- Press the save button.

Click Edit to edit or delete the alarm.

# Buy books and audiobooks from Apple Books on your iPad

In the Books application, you can find today's bestsellers, check out the top chart, or browse lists compiled by Apple Books publishers. When you select a book or audiobook, you can listen to or read it in the application.

- Open Books, click on Book Store or audiobooks to view the names, or click the Search button to search for a specific name, genre, or author.
- Click on the cover of a book to see more information, read a copy, listen to a preview, or check if you want to read it.

- Touch Buy to get the book or click Get to download a book that is free.

# Download or Buy an application from the App Store

In the Apps Store application, you can find new applications, personal stories, tips & tricks, and activities within the app.

## To look for applications

Click on one of the following to see the applications, games & activities within the app:

- Today: check out the stories, programs, and events in an app.
- Games: find the next game in dozens of categories, which include action, fun experience, puzzles, race, etc.
- App: find new releases, check out the top charts, or browse using Category.
- Arcade.
- Search: Enter what you want, then touch the Search icon on your keyboard.

Touch an application, tap on the price or touch Get if the application is free, then adhere to the directives on your display to download the application

# CUSTOMIZE YOUR DEVICE

## Set sound options

Set options for alarm, ringtones, etc. on your device

- Enter the setting application, tap on Sound.
- Move the slide to change the volume.
- Touch Ringtone & other options to choose sounds for the ringing tone & alert tones.

## Silent your device

To mute calls, notifications, and sounds effects for some time, open the Control Center, touch the Focus button, and touch Do Not Disturb.

## Change the wallpaper on your device

On your device, use a picture or image as your Lock or Home screen wallpaper. You can pick from still & dynamic images.

- Enter the Settings application> Wallpaper> pick a New Wallpaper.
- Do any of the below:

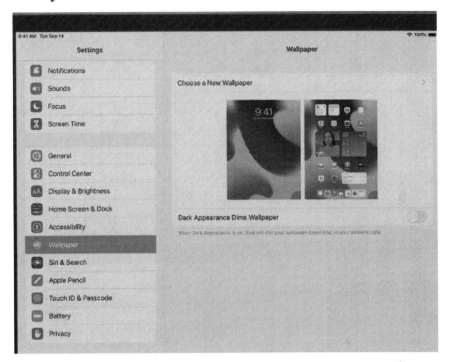

> Select the default image in the group at the upper part of your display.

> Select one of your pictures (touch an album, then touch the picture).

> Touch the Parallax Effect button to open the Perspective Zoom, which makes your wallpaper look like it's "moving" when you change the viewing angle.

4. Touch Set, and select any of the below:
   - ➢ Set as home screen
   - ➢ Set as lock screen
   - ➢ Both

# Adjust the brightness and color of your iPad

On your device, you can dim the display or make it brighter.

To make your iPad screen brighter or dimmer, do any of the below:

- Launch the Controls Centre, and then slide the light button ☼.
- Enter the Settings application> Display and Brightness, then slide the slider.

To adjust the brightness automatically, enter the settings application, tap on Accessibility, touch Display and Text Size, and activate Auto-Brightness.

## Activate or deactivate dark mode

The Dark mode gives your device a dark colour scheme that meets the lighting conditions of your surroundings. When Dark Mode is active, you can use your iPad to read in bed, without worrying about disturbing those people around you.

Do any of the below:

- Launch the Controls Center, press & hold the Light button ☼, and touch the Dark mode button ◑ to activate or deactivate the dark mode.
- Enter the Settings application, touch Display and Brightness, then choose Dark to activate the Dark mode or light to deactivate it.

## Activate or deactivate True Tone

True Tone automatically adjusts the color & intensity of the screen to fit the lighting around you.

Do any of the below:

- Launch the Control Center, press & hold the Light button ☼, and then press the True Tone button ☀ to activate or deactivate true tone.

- Enter the Setting application> Display & Brightness, and enable or disable True Tone.

## Change the iPad's name

You can change your device's name, which is used by AirDrop, iCloud, your Personal Hotspot, and your PC.

- Enter the Settings application> General> About> Name.
- Touch the Clear Text button ⊗, type a new name, & touch Done.

## Change the time & date on the iPad

- Enter the Setting application> General> Date & Time.
- Activate any of the below:
  - ➢ Set Automatically: your device would receive the exact time via the network and updates it for your time zone.
  - ➢ 24 Hours: your device would display 0 to 23 Hours

# Change the language and region on your device

- Enter the Settings application> General> Languages and regions.
- Set any of the below:
  - ➢ iPad Language
  - ➢ Region
  - ➢ Format of the calendar
  - ➢ Temperature unit (Celsius or Fahrenheit)
- To add keyboard in a different language, enter the Settings application> General> Keyboard> Keyboard and touch add a new keyboard.

# Create a folder in the Home Screen

- Hold down any of the applications on your Home screen, and touch Edit Home Screen.
  The applications would start jiggling.
- You can create a folder by dragging an application onto another application.
- You can add other applications to the folder by dragging the apps into the folder.

- Press & hold the folder to rename it, touch Rename, and type the new name.

  If the applications start jiggling, touch the Home screen background & try once more.

- When you are done, touch Done, and double-tap the background of the Home screen.

To delete a folder, touch the folder and open it, then remove all the applications by dragging them out of the folder. The folder would automatically be erased.

## Move applications & widgets around your device

- Press & hold any application or widget on your Home screen, and then touch the **Edit Home screen** button.

  The items would start jiggling.

- Drag the widget or application to any of the locations below:

- somewhere else on that page

- Another home screen page

  You can move an application to another Home Screen page by dragging the application to the right edge of your display. You may have to wait a second for the next page to show. The dots on the dock indicate the number of pages and which ones you are viewing.

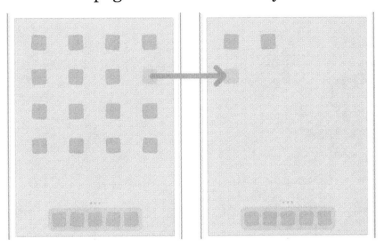

- When you're done, touch Done at the upper right part of the screen.

## Reset the Home Screen & applications to their original appearance

- Enter the Settings application> General> Transfer or reset iPad.
- Touch Reset, touch Reset the Home screen layout and click on the Reset button.

Any folders you create are deleted and your downloaded applications are sorted alphabetically after applications that come with the iPad.

## Uninstall applications

Do any of the below:

- Remove an application from the Home screen: Hold down the application on your Home Screen, touch Remove Application, then touch Remove app from Home Screen, or click Delete application to remove it from the iPad.

- Remove an application from the application library and on the Home screen: Hold down the application in the application library, click the Delete application button, and click Delete

  You can download the applications you have uninstalled anytime you like.

## Add & organize controls in the control centre

- Enter the Settings application, and tap on Control Center.

- To add or erase a control, click  or ⊖ beside a control.

- To change the location of a control, touch ≡ beside the control and drag it to a new location.

## Change or lock your iPad orientation

Many applications have a different look when your device is rotated.

You can lock the orientation of your screen so that it does not change whenever you rotate your device

Launch the Controls Centre, and touch the "Lock" button

🔒 .

After locking the screen orientation, the Orientation Lock

icon 🔒 appears in its status bar.

# FOCUS

The Focus feature helps you to focus on a task by reducing distractions. When you need to focus on or step away from your device, Focus can mute all your notifications temporarily or leave only a few notifications (e.g., related to the task you are performing) and let other people and the applications know that you have work to do.

You can pick from a catalog of available focus options or setup your own.

**Note:** To quickly mute notifications, launch the Controls Centre, touch the Focus button, and tap on Do Not Disturb.

## Setup a Focus

If you want to focus on a specific task, you can customize the Focus options provided, such as DND, Personal, Sleep or Work or you can setup a Custom Focus. You can turn off notifications or allow notifications from people and applications relevant to your Course, for example, you can setup a Work Focus and let only notifications from your colleagues and applications you need for the work.

Similarly, you can personalize a home screen page, which would have applications related to Focus, and make the page the one thing you can access when you activate the Focus.

- Enter the Settings application, tap on Focus.
- Touch a Focus, for example, DND, Work, Sleep, or Personal, and then adhere to the directives on your display.

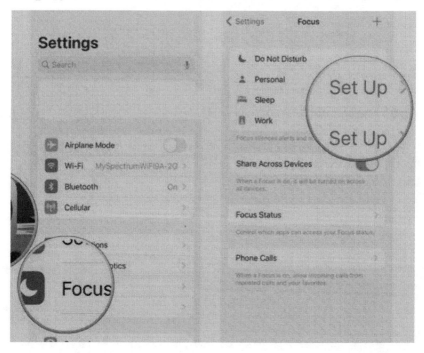

## Create a Focus

You can create a Custom Focus if you want to focus on something different from the given Focus modes.

- Enter the Settings application, tap on Focus.

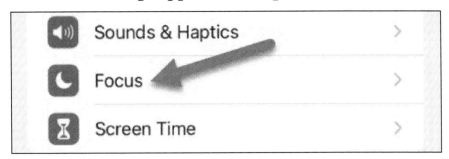

- Touch the Add button ┼ at the upper right part of your display, and touch Custom.

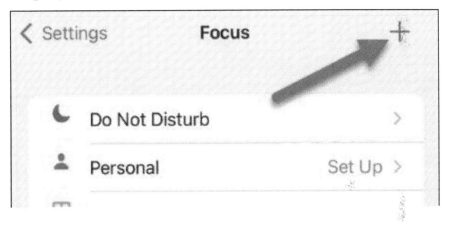

- Label the Focus, and touch Return.
- Select a colour & icon to indicate your Focus, and then touch the "Next" button.
- Tap on the **Add Person** button to select the people you want to get notifications from when Focus mode is activated.

---

- You can decide to get calls from **Everybody, Nobody, Favourites** or **All Contacts.**

- You can also decide to allow Repeated calls.

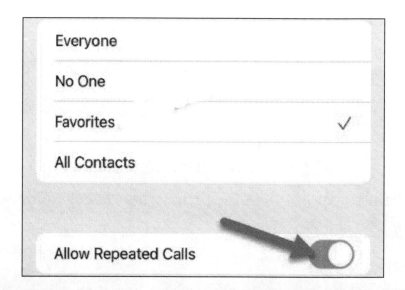

- Touch Allow [X] people or do not allow.

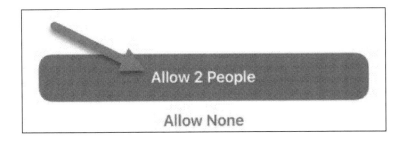

- On the next display, touch **Add App** to pick the applications you want to get alerts from when the Focus mode is activated.

- Touch the Allow [X] Applications or Allow None button.

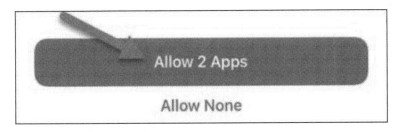

- On the next display, decide if want to **Allow Time-Sensitive notification** when Focus is active, or you can touch **Not Now**.

- Touch Done to create the Custom Focus.

Once your personal focus has been created, you can change the Settings by opening the settings application -> Focus and choosing the name of the Focus.

## Allow calls from emergency contacts

- Open the contact application.
- Choose a contact, and touch Edit.
- Touch a Ringing tone or Text tone, and activate Emergency Bypass.

## Activate a Focus mode from the Controls Centre

- Open the Controls Centre, touch the **Focus** button and touch the Focus you want to activate (for instance, DND).

- To select an end point for a Focus mode, touch beside the Focus mode, choose an option (like 1 hour or till I leave this location) and then touch 😶 once more.

Your friends will see that you have muted the notification, but they can notify you if there is an emergency.

## Schedule a Focus to automatically activate

You can programme Focus to activate at a certain time, location, or when you are making use of a certain application.

- Enter the Settings application> Focus, then touch the Focus you want.
- Touch Automation or Add Schedule, and then specify the time, location, or application you want to activate the Focus.
- To automatically activate this Focus based on application usage, location, etc. touch Smart Activation, activate Smart Activation, then touch ❮ at the upper part of your display.

## Deactivate a Focus mode

Once you are done with a Focus, you can quickly disable it.

- Do any of the below:
  - ➤ Hold down the Focus icon on your lock screen.
  - ➤ Launch the Controls Centre, then press the Focus button.
- Touch the active Focus to deactivate it.

## Delete a Focus

If you no longer need a Focus you created, you can delete it.

- Enter the Settings application> Focus.
- Touch the Focus, scroll down, and then touch the Delete Focus button.

# BACKUP & RESTORE YOUR IPAD

## Backup iPad

You can backup your device with iCloud or your PC.

Tip: If you are buying a new iPad, you can use backup to transfer your data to the new device.

### Backup your iPad via iCloud

- Enter the Settings application> [your name]> iCloud> iCloud Back up.
- Activate iCloud Back up.
  iCloud would automatically backup your iPad every day when it's locked, connected to power & Wi-Fi.
  **Note**: With WiFi + Cellular model, your network system allows you to backup your iPad through your mobile network. Enter the Settings application> [your name]> iCloud> iCloud Backup, & activate or deactivate Backup Over Cellular.
- Tap on **Back up Now** to make a manual back up.

To view your iCloud backups, enter the Settings application> [your name]> iCloud> Manage Storage>

Back up. To erase a backup, pick the backup from the catalog & tap on Delete Backup.

Note: If you activate an iCloud feature (like iCloud Photos or Contacts) in the Settings application> [your name]> iCloud, its data is saved in iCloud. Since the info is automatically stored on all of your devices, it is not added to your iCloud back up.

## Backup iPad with your Mac

- Connect your iPad and computer by cable.
- In your Mac Finder side bar, choose your iPad. MacOS 10.15 or later is required to use Finder.
- At the upper part of the Finder window, tap on "General".
- Choose **Backup all the data on iPad to Mac**.
- If you want your back up to be protected with a passcode, choose **Encrypt local back up**.
- Tap on Backup Now.

## Backup your device with a Windows computer

- Connect your iPad & computer by cable.
- In the iTunes application on your PC, tap on the iPad button close to the upper left part of the iTunes window.
- Tap on Summary.
- Tap on Backup Now(under Backups).
- If you want your backups to be encrypted, choose **Encrypt local back up**, enter your password and click the Set Password button.

To check out the backup you have stored on your computer, choose Edit> Preference and click on Device.


## Restore Backed up contents to your iPad

You can restore settings, contents, & applications from a backup to a new or recently erased iPad.


### Restore iPad from an iCloud backup

- Switch on your new or recently erased iPad.
- Adhere to the directives to select a language & region.
- Touch Setup Manually.

- Touch Restore from iCloud Backup to restore and adhere to the directives on your screen.

## Restore your device from a computer backup

- With a USB cable, connect a new or recently erased iPad to the PC that has your backup.
- Do any of the below:
  - ➢ In your Mac's Finder side bar: Choose your iPad and click the Trust button.
    MacOS 10.15 or later is required to use Finder to restore the iPad from a backup.
  - ➢ In the iTunes application on a Windows computer: If more than one device is connected to your computer, click the device icon close to the upper left part of the iTunes window, and choose your new or recently erased iPad from the catalog.
- On the Welcome display, tap on the **Restore from this backup** button, choose your back up from the catalog and tap on the "Continue" button.

If the backup is encrypted, you have to insert the password before you can restore your settings & files.

# CAMERA

Learn how to take great pictures with the camera application on your tablet. Select from camera modes like Photos Pan & Square, & utilize special camera features like Live & Burst Pictures.

## Take a picture

As a rule, you see Photo mode when you launch the camera application. Swipe the mode selector down or up to pick another mode, like video, pane, etc.

- Tap the camera icon to launch the camera application.
- Touch the Shutter to capture a photo, or press any of the Volume buttons.

Press the Flash button to switch on or off the lights, and then select Auto, On, or Off.

To zoom in or out, simply pinch your display.

# Capture panoramic pictures

- Select Pano mode, then touch the Shutter.
- Move slowly in the arrow's direction, and ensure the arrow stays in the middle line.

- When you are done, touch the Shutter button once more.

Touch the arrows to move in the other direction. Rotate your device to landscape orientation to pan vertically.

## Take a selfie

- Change the camera to the Front Camera by touch the Flip camera button 🔄 or 📷 .
- Place your device in front of you.
- Touch the Shutter or any of the Volume buttons.

## Take Photos with Burst Mode

Burst mode captures many high-speed pictures, so there are several shots to select from. You can take Burst pictures with the front & back cameras.

- Select Square or Photo mode.
- Press & hold the Shutter button to take multiple fast pictures.
  The counter would show the number of photos taken.
- Raise your finger to end the shots.
- To choose the pictures you want to save, touch the Burst thumb-nail, and choose the Select button.
- Touch the Circle in the bottom right part of every picture you plan on saving as a single picture, then touch Done.

Click on the thumbnail then click the eteok button 🗑 to delete the whole set of burst images.

---

## Take a Live Picture

A live picture takes what happens before & after the picture, as well as the sounds.

- Select Photo mode.
- Click the Live Photo button◉ to activate the feature (yellow is on).
- Touch the Shutter to take a picture.

In your Albums, Live Pictures are labeled with **Live** in the upper left part of your display.

## Record a video

- Select video mode.
- Touch the record button, or press any of the volume buttons to start recording and press it to stop recording.

## Record a slow-motion video

After recording a Slow motion video, you record the video as usual and when you play it again, you see that the effect is slow.

- Select Slo-mo mode.
- Touch the record button, or press any of the volume buttons to start and end the recording.

To play a part of the video in slow motion and play the rest at normal speed, touch the thumb-nail and then touch Edit. Drag the vertical bars under the frame viewer to determine the segment you want to be played in slow motion.

To edit the slow-motion setting, enter the Settings application> Camera> Record Slo-mo

## Take a Timelapse video

- Select Timelapse mode.
- Position your device where you want to capture the timelapse video, like a traffic flowing, sunset, or other experiences over a period.
- To record, press the Record button; press again to end the recording.

# View your pictures

- In the Camera application, touch the thumb nail picture under the Shutter button.
- Swipe to the right to view the pictures you have taken lately.

  Touch your display to show or conceal the controls.
- Touch All Photos to view all the pictures & videos you saved in the Photos application.

# Share your pictures

- When checking out a picture, touch the Share button[⬆]·
- To share your pictures, choose an option, such as AirDrop, Mail, or Messages.

# Scan QR codes with your camera

You can use the Camera or code scanner to view Quick Response (QR) codes for links to sites, applications, tickets, etc. your device camera automatically detects & displays the QR code.

- Open the camera and then place the iPad in a way that the code shows on your display.
- Touch the notification that shows up on your display to go to the appropriate site or application.

# FACETIME

You can utilize the Face-Time application to stay in touch with your friends and family, whether they use Apple, Android, or Windows devices. With the spatial voice feature in Face-Time, people on the phone talk to you from where they are on the screen and it feels like they are in the same room with you.

## Setup FaceTime

- Enter the Settings application> FaceTime, and activate FaceTime.
- Do any of the below:
  - ➤ Setup an account for your FaceTime calls: Touch **Use your Apple ID on FaceTime**, and touch Sign In.
  - ➤ Highlight the speaker on the call: **Activate Speaking**.
  - ➤ Capture a Live Picture in a FaceTime call: Activate FaceTime Live photos.

# Create a link to make a FaceTime Call

Create a link & send it to one or more persons with Mail or Messaging, which they can utilize to be part of the FaceTime call.

You can invite anybody to participate in a FaceTime call, even people who don't have Apple devices. They can join the call with their web browser.

- Touch the Create Link button at the upper part of your display.
- Select an option to send the link (Mail, Messages, etc.).

## Make & get Face Time calls

Turn off your video

Turn off your mic.

With an Internet connection, you can make & get calls on Face Time.

## Make FaceTime Calls

- In the FaceTime application, touch New FaceTime at the upper of your display.

- Type the number or name you plan on calling in the search box, and touch Face Time video  or voice call .

  Or, you can touch the Add Contact button ⊕ to open Contacts and then start your call.

## Receive Calls

When a Face-Time call arrives, do any of the below:

— Send the caller a text message.

Set up a reminder to return a call.

- Answer Call: tap on Accept.
- Reject a call: Touch Decline.

- Create a reminder to call again: Touch Remind Me.
- Send an SMS to the caller: Click message.

## Initiate a Face Time call from a text message

In a messaging chat, you can begin a Face Time call with the person you are talking to.

- Press the FaceTime button ⬜◁ in the upper right corner of the message chat.
- Do any of the below:
  - ➢ Click the FaceTime Audio button.
  - ➢ Click on the FaceTime video.

## Take a Live picture while on a Face Time call

When you make a Face Time video call, you can take a Live Picture to snap a moment of the call. The camera snaps what takes place before & after the picture, as well as the sound, so you can view & listen to it as it happened.

To capture a live photo with FaceTime Live, first, ensure FaceTime Live is activated in the Settings application> FaceTime, then do any of the below:

- Single person call: Tap the capture button $\bigcirc$.
- In a Group call: Click the person's tile, click the Full-Screen button ⬉, and then touch the Take Photo button $\bigcirc$.

## Start a FaceTime Group call

In the FaceTime application, you can have about 32 people participating in a Group FaceTime call.

- Touch New Face Time.
- Enter the numbers or names of the individuals you want to participate in the call in the input box.

  You can also click the Add Contact button ⊕ to open your contact list and then add a person. Or click on the contacts shown in your call history.

- Touch the FaceTime button ⬛◁ to make a video call, or press the Audio key to make a FaceTime Audio call 📞.

Everybody participating in the call would appear in a tile on your display.

## Add someone to the call

All participants can add other people at any time while the FaceTime call is ongoing.

Tap to add more
people to the call.

- While a FaceTime call is going on, touch your display to see the controls (if not visible), click on the controls, and then click the Add Person button.
- Enter the number, Apple ID, or name, of the individual you want to add in the login box at the top.

  Alternatively, click the Add button ⊕ to add one of your Contacts.
- Touch Add People.

## Activate Centre Stage

The Center Stage feature adjusts the front-facing camera to frame you even when you are moving around the stage while the call is going on.

- While on a Face Time call, Open the Controls Centre.
- Touch **Video Effect**, then touch Center Stage activate it.
  Touch it again to deactivate Center Stage.


## Blur the background

You can activate Portrait Mode, which blurs your background & make you the focus of the call.

- While making a FaceTime call, touch your tile.
- Touch the cluttered back button on your tile.
  Press the button once more to switch it off.

You can also activate Portrait mode in the Controls Centre. Open the Controls Center, then touch Video Effects.

# Go to the rear camera

While making a FaceTime video call, touch your tile, then touch the Flip camera button ⟳.

To return to the Front camera, press the Button again.

# Turn off the camera

While on a FaceTime call, touch the screen to display the controls, and then click the Video button ▢◁. (Click again to turn on the camera.)

# Filter out background noise

If you want people to hear you clearly and other sounds filtered out, you can enable the Voice isolation mode. This feature singles out your voice on FaceTime calls while blocking ambient noise.

During a FaceTime call, Open the Controls Centre, click the Mic Mode button, and then choose Voice Insulation.

# Add sound in your surroundings

If you want people to hear your voice as well as the sounds in your surroundings while on a FaceTime call, you can activate the Wide Spectrum mode.

During a FaceTime call, open the Controls Centre, touch the Mic Mode button, and then choose Wide Spectrum.

# Turn the sound off

While on a FaceTime call, touch your screen to display the FaceTime controls, then press the Voice button 🎤 to mute the sound.

Press the button again to activate the sound.

# Block unwanted Face Time callers

- In your FaceTime history, click the Information button ⓘ beside the contact's name, number, or e-mail.
- Scroll down, touch block this caller, and touch Contact.
- Choose the contacts you plan to block.

# Use filters to change your appearance

- While on a FaceTime call, touch your tile, and then touch the effects button.

- Touch the Filters button to open the filters.

- Tap any of the filters at the lower part of your display to change your looks.

# SIRI

Talking to Siri is an easy way to get stuff done on your device. You could tell Siri to translate a sentence, set alarm, finding a place, give a weather report, etc.

For Siri to perform some tasks your device needs to be online.

Response from Siri

Tap to continue speaking to Siri.

## Setup Siri

If you did not setup Siri when setting up your device, Enter the Settings application> Siri and Search, then do any of the below:

- If you want to use your voice to Call Siri: Enable Listen for **Hey Siri**.
- Summon Siri using a button: Activate Press Top Button for Siri.

# Call Sir with your voice

After activating **Listen for Hey Siri**

- Say **Hey Siri** and state your request.
  For instance, you could say, **Hey Siri, how is the weather today?**.
- If you want to make another request, say **Hey Siri** again or click on the **Listen** button.

# Call Siri with a button

- Long press the top button.
- When Siri shows up, state your request
- Tap on the Listen button to make another request.

# Make corrections if Siri does not understand you

- Repeat your request: Click the Listen button, and state your request differently.
- Spell some of your requests: Click the Listen button, then repeat your request by spelling words that Siri

does not understand. For instance, say "Call" and then spell out the name of the Person.

- Edit before sending a message: Say **Change it**.
- Use text to edit your request: If your request is displayed on your screen, you can edit it. Touch the request, and edit it with your keyboard.

## Write instead of talking to Siri

- Enter the Settings application> Accessibility> Siri, and activate Type to Siri.
- To ask Siri a question, summon Siri, and utilize your Keyboard to type what you want Siri to do for you.

## Have Siri announce calls

Siri detects incoming FaceTime calls, that you can answer & reject through your voice.

- Enter the Settings application> Siri and Search> Announce Call, then select an option.

- When the call arrives, Siri would identify the caller & would ask if you would love to answer the call. Say **yes** to take the call, or **no** to reject it.

## Change Siri settings on iPad

Enter the Settings application> Siri and Search, then do any of the below:

- Block access to Siri when the iPad is locked: Deactivate Allow Siri when locked.
- Change the language that Siri responds to: Click on a language, and then choose another language.
- Change Siri's voice: Touch Siri Voice, then select another type or voice.
- Always view Siri's response on your display: Touch Siri Responses, and activate Always Display Siri's Caption.
- View your request on the screen: Click Siri's Response, and activate Always Display Speech.

# APPLE PAY

Setup Apple Pay to make safe payments in applications & sites that are compatible with Apple Pay.

## Add a card

- Enter the Settings application> Wallet and Apple Pay.
- Click the Add Card button. You might be told to login using an Apple ID.
- Do any of the below:
  - ➤ Add a new card: arrange your device in a way that your card shows up in the frame, or manually type the card information.
  - ➤ Add your old card: Choose the card associated with the Apple ID, the cards you utilize with Apple Pay on your other devices, or the card you removed. Press the Continue button, then enter the CVV card number.

The issuer of the card would decide if your card is qualified for Apple Pay & might request for more details.

# View your card's information and change the card's settings

- Enter the Settings application> Wallet and Apple Pay.
- Touch a card and change what you want

## Change your Apple Pay settings

- Enter the Settings application> Wallet and Apple Pay.
- Do any of the below:
  - ➢ Choose your default card
  - ➢ Add the shipping address & purchase information.

# Pay in the application, in an Application clip, or on the internet

- While checking out, touch the Apple Pay button.
- Go through your payment details.
  You can change your credit card, payment and shipping addresses, and personal information.
- Complete the payment, by authenticating with Touch ID or entering your password.

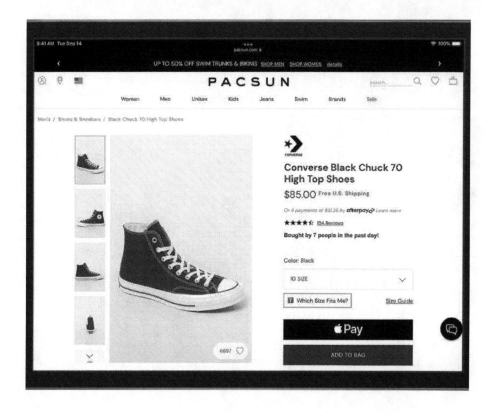

# ICLOUD

iCloud keeps your pictures, videos, docs, backups, etc. secure and automatically updated on all your devices. iCloud would give you 5 GB of free storage & an email account. You can sign up with iCloud + for more storage & features.

## Change your iCloud settings

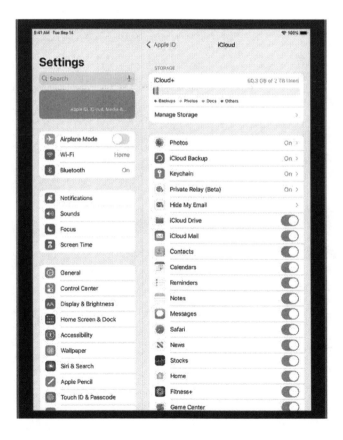

- Enter the Settings application> [your name]> iCloud.
- Do any of the below:
  - ➢ Check the status of your iCloud storage.
  - ➢ Activate the applications & features you plan on making use of, like mail, pictures, messages, & contacts.

## Setup iCloud Drive on iPad

Utilize the Files application to save files & folders on iCloud Drive.

### Activate iCloud Drive

Enter the settings application, tap on (your name), touch iCloud, and activate iCloud Drive

### Select which applications utilize iCloud Drive

Enter the Settings application> [your name]> iCloud, then activate or deactivate every application list under iCloud Drive.

### Browse iCloud Drive

- In the Files application
- Click the "Browse" button at the lower part of your display.
- Under Location, touch iCloud Drive

  If you can't find Locations, touch Browse once more. If you can't find iCloud Drive in Locations, touch Location.
- Click on a folder to open it.

## Upgrade, change or cancel your iCloud + subscription

- Enter the Settings application> [your name]> iCloud.
- Click on Manage Storage, touch change the Storage Plan, then choose an option & adhere to the directives on your display.

Note: If you cancel your iCloud + subscription, you will not be able to access the additional iCloud storage.

# SAFARI

In the Safari application, insert a URL or a search term to look for sites or certain info.

See your
Bookmarks,
Reading List,
and Tab Groups.

Enter a web
address, search, or
quickly access your
Favorites.

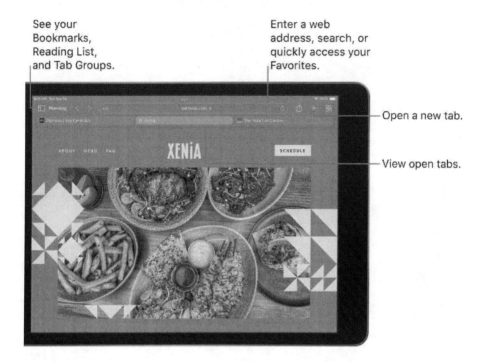

Open a new tab.

View open tabs.

## Search the internet

- In the search box at the upper part of your screen, enter a URL, phrase, or a search term
- Touch one of the search suggestions or touch **Go** on the keyboard to search what you wrote.

# Search the webpage

You can look for a word or phrase on the page you are on.

- Click the Share button ⬆, then touch Find on the page.
- Enter what you want to look for in the search box.
- Click the "Next Page Results" button ⌄ to see more examples.

# Navigate a page in Safari

You can surf around a page with a few clicks.

- Back to top: touch the top edge of your display twice quickly return to the beginning of a long page.
- View more of the webpage: Rotate your device to Landscape Orientation.
- Refresh the webpage: Drag down from the webpage top.
- Share links: Touch the share button ⬆ on the upper right part of your page.

# View two pages in Split View

- Open a blank page in Split View: long-press the Expose button 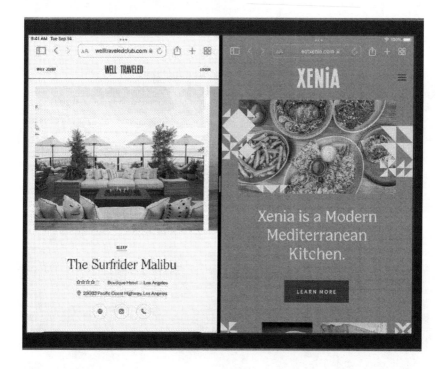, then touch New Split View window.

- Open the link in Split View: Hold down the link, then touch open it in Split View.

- Move a window to another side of Split View: hold down the Safari Multitasking Controls button ••• at the upper part of the window, and then move it by dragging it to the right or left.

- Close a tab in a split view window: Long press the Expose button.

---

- Exit Split View: move the divider over the window you plan on closing by dragging it.

## Translating a Page

If you come across a site in a different language, Safari can help you translate the text.

When you see a site in a different language, click the Format settings button AA and if there is a translation, click the Translate button.

## Personalize the start page

Each time you open a new page you start on the Start page. You can personalize the Startpage with new background options & images.

- Touch ╋ in the upper right part of your display to open the new tab.
- Scroll down, and touch the Edit button.
- Select an option for the home page.

# Change the text size

- Touch the Page Settings button AA on the left part of the search box.
- Touch the larger A button to increase the font size, or the small A button to reduce it.

# Change the screen and custom controls

Utilize the View menu to enter the reader's view, hide the search box, set privacy controls for a site, etc.

Click the Page Settings button AA on the left part of the search box, the do any of the below:

- Go through the page without advertisements or a navigation menu: Click Show Reader View (if any).
- Conceal the search box: Touch Hide Tool bar (click at the top of your display to reveal it).
- Check the mobile version of the website: Touch Request a mobile website (if any).

# Bookmark the webpage you are in

- Touch ⬆️ on the search box.
- Touch the Add Bookmark button.

## Bookmark open tabs

- Pinch Close with 3 of your fingers to see your tabs.
- Long-press one of your tabs, then touch Add Bookmarks for the (number of) Tabs.

## View and organize your bookmarks

- Touch the sidebar button ⬜ to view the groups of Tabs.
- Click on the Bookmark button 🔖.
- Click Edit to create new folders or delete, rename or sort bookmarks.
- Touch Done to save the changes.

## Add a page to your Favourites

- Open the page, click the Share button ⬆️, and then click the Add to Favorites button.

- To edit your favorites, click the sidebar button⊞, click Bookmarks. Click Favorites, click the Edit button to rearrange, change the name, or delete your Favourites.

To view your Favourites, click the Sidebar button⊞, and then scroll down and click Favorites or Reading Lists.

## Add a site icon to your device Home screen

You can add a site icon to your iPad home screen to quickly access that page.

From the page, click the Share button⬆, and then touch add to the Home screen.

The icon will only appear on the device you are adding it to.

## Visit websites without making history

On the iPad, you can use the Private Browsing mode to open private tabs, which would not show on your device History.

Click the Display sidebar button ⬚, and click the Private button.

To hide a page & leave the Private Browsing mode, click the sidebar button ⬚ and move to another Tab group. The address appears the next time you utilize Private Browsing.

# TRANSLATE APP

You can translate text, audio, and conversation between the languages supported in the translation application. You can also download languages for full translations on your iPad without having to connect to the internet.

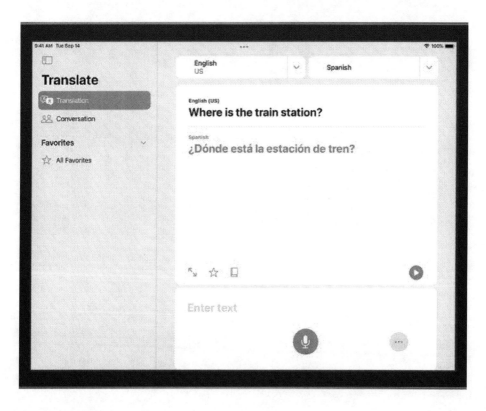

## Translate your text or voice

- Touch Translation, choose the language to translate it, and do any of the below:
  - ➤ Click the **Enter text** button, write the phrase and click the **Go** button.
  - ➤ Click the Listen button 🔘, then say the phrase.
- When the translation appears, do any of the below:
  - ➤ Play the translation: press the Play key ▶.
  - ➤ Store what you have translated to your Favourites: click the Favourites button ☆.
  - ➤ Click the dictionary button 📖, then click a word to find its definition.
  - ➤ Show the translation to others: Press the Enter Full-Screen button ⤢.

## Translate a conversation

Your device displays a text bubble translated on both sides of the conversation. You can download languages so that you can translate when you are offline or the on-device mode is activated.

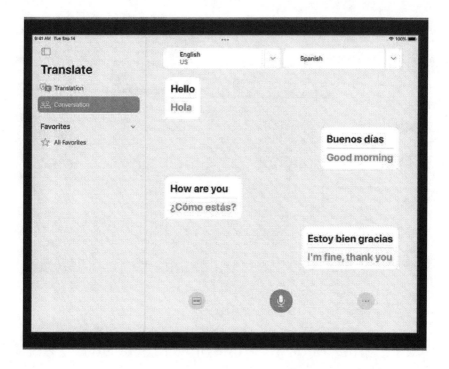

- Touch Conversations.

- Click the Listen button, then talk in one of the 2 languages.

You can interpret a conversation without having to press the microphone before speaking. Click the More Options button ***, click the Auto Translate button, and then click the Listen button to start the conversation. The iPad automatically detects when you start talking and when you are done speaking.

When you're chatting face -to -face, click the "Chat" button ▬▬ and then touch the "Face to Face" button so everyone can see their side.

## Download languages for offline translation or Device mode

If there is no Internet connection or the on-device mode is activated, you can use downloaded languages to translate your conversation.

- Enter the Settings application> Translate.
- Click Downloaded languages, and then click the Download button ⊕ beside the languages you plan to download.
- Activate On-device mode.

## Translate text in pictures

When viewing a picture that has text, click the text key ⌗, choose the text you want to translate, touch the Translate icon.

---

# Translate in the Camera application

- Open the Camera application, and set the iPad so that the text appears on your display.

- When a yellow frame shows up around the text, click the Define Text button ⬚.

- Choose the text you plan to translate and touch the Translate icon.

# APPLE PENCIL

## Pair your 2ⁿᵈ Gen Apple pencil to your iPad

To pair your Apple Pencil to your device simply attach the Pencil to the magnetic connector on the right part of the iPad.

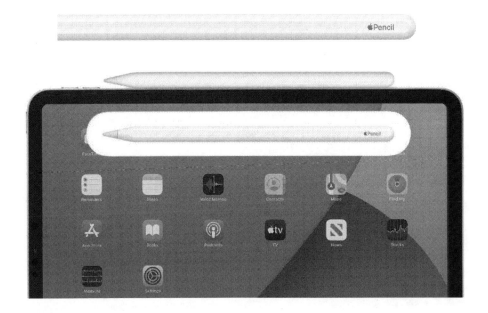

## Charge your Apple Pencil

- Ensure Bluetooth is enabled in the Settings application> Bluetooth.

- Place the Apple pencil on the right part of your device where the magnetic connector is.

## Use Apple Pencil to insert text in any text field

1. Use your Apple Pencil to write in a text field & Scribble would convert what you have written to typed text.
2. Touch the Scribble bar to use the shortcut.

   Available options depend on the application you are making use of, including undo keys ⟲, the display Keyboard keys ⌨, etc.

   When you insert text, press the Ellipsis button ⦙ to automatically minimize the tool bar, and activate Auto-minimize.

## Select & review the text with Apple Pencil

When entering text with Scribble & Apple Pencil, you can:

- Delete a word by scratching the word out.
- Enter text by holding down the text field, and writing in the text field that opens.

- Add or separate symbols by drawing a vertical line between the characters.
- Highlight text by drawing a circle round the text or underlining the text to highlight it & view editing options.
- Highlight a word: tap the word two times.
- Highlight a paragraph: tap a word in the paragraph three times, or use the Apple Pencil to drag over the paragraph.

## Deactivate Scribble

Enter the Settings application> Apple Pencil, and deactivate Scribble.

## Take a screenshot with your Apple Pencil

You can use Apple Pencil to quickly capture your iPad's display, and share it with others, or utilize it as a document.

- To take a screenshot, use the Apple Pencil to swipe up from any of the two corners at the bottom of your device.

- Markup the screen shot with your Apple Pencil. Utilize the Markup tool bar at the lower part of your display to switch the drawing tools.

- To send the screenshot to someone (like in a message) or to save it in a file (like in a note), click the Share button ⬆, then select an option.

- When you are done, press the Done button, and then select an option.

# MAIL

## Setup an email account

- Enter the Settings application> Mail> Account> Add Account.
- Do any of the below:
  - ➤ Touch an e-mail service - for instance, Microsoft Exchange or iCloud - and enter your e-mail account details.
  - ➤ Touch Other, touch the Add Mail Account button, and enter your details to setup a new account.

Follow these steps to add more accounts


## Send an email

In the Mail application, you can write & edit e-mail from any of your accounts.

### To write an e-mail message

- Press the compose button ☑ .
- Touch the insertion point in the e-mail, then type your message.

- Touch Aa to change your format, which includes font style, text colour, etc.

Change mailboxes
or accounts.

Delete, move, or mark
multiple messages.

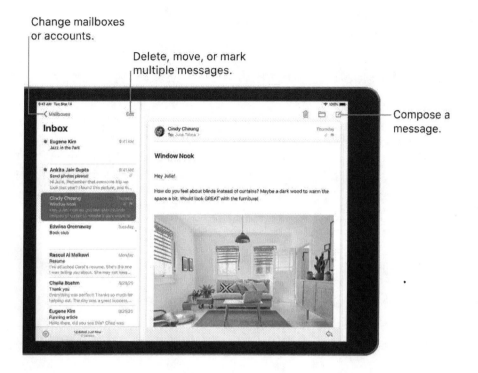

Compose a
message.

## Add Recipients

- Tap on the **TO** field, then enter the recipients' names.

  You can also click the Add Contact button ⊕ to open contact and add a recipient from there.

- If you are sending a copy, click on the Cc / Bcc field and do any of the below:

  ➢ Touch the cc box, and enter the individuals' names you want to send a copy to.

> ➢ Click on the Bcc field, and enter the names of the individuals you do not want other recipients to see.

## Reply an e-mail

- Click on the Email, click More Actions ↰, and then click Reply.
- Write your reply

## Add documents to your e-mail

You can add saved files to an e-mail.

- Click on the email you want to attach the file to, then click the Add Doc button ⬒ at the top of your keyboard.
- Find the files in the Files application, and touch the file to put it in your e-mail.

  In the Files application, click on the Recent or Browse button at the lower part of your display, and then click on a folder, location, or file to open it.

## Upload a saved photo or video

- In the e-mail you want to upload a picture or video to, click the Upload Image button ⬚ on the keyboard, and then click the Photo Library button ⬚.

- Find the picture or video in the image selector.
- Click on a photo or video to add it to your email.

## Take a picture or video to add an email

- Click where you want to put the picture or video, then click the Picture button ⬚ at the top of the keyboard.
- Click on Take a video or photo, then execute.
- Click Use the image or use the video to add it to your email, or click on Retake if you want to take the shot again.

## Scan a document into an e-mail

- In the e-mail you want to add the scanned file to, click the Scan Toolbar button ⬚ at the top of your keyboard.
- Set the iPad so that the doc page shows on your display, your device would copy the page automatically.

  To take the page manually, click the "Take a picture" button ⬚. Press the Flash Setup button ⚡ to turn the light on or off.

---

- Scan more pages, click Save when you are done.

## Look for text in an e-mail

- Swipe down from the center of the mail-box to open the search box.
- Click the search box and enter the text you are looking for.
- Select from search mailbox or current mailbox at the top of the results list.
- Click an e-mail in the result list to check it out.

## Delete an email

When viewing an email: press the delete button 🗑 (at the top or bottom of your display, depending on the size and direction of the screen).

# NOTES

You can utilize the Notes application to quickly write thoughts or organize information with check lists, photos, Internet links, scanned documents, handwritten notes, etc.

## Create & Format a new note

- Touch the new Note button , then type your text.

- Touch Aa to change the format.

- Click **Done** to save the note.

To add a checklist to your note click on the Checklist button ⊘—, and type what you want, then touch return to go to the next item

To add a table to your note, click on the Table button ⊞

## Draw or write in a note

- Start to draw or write with your Apple Pencil. Or to write or draw using your finger, touch the Manuscript button Ⓐ.

- Change colors or materials: Use the Mark-up tools.

- When writing with Apple Pencil, change your handwritten text to typed text: Click the handwriting tool Ⓐ (on the left side of the pen), and then begin to write.

## Add photos or videos

- In the note, click the Camera key 📷.

- Picture a video or picture from the photos library, or snap one.

- To edit an attachment's preview size, hold down the attachment, and then touch Large image or Small image.

Tip: To draw on an image, click on the image, and then press the Markup button Ⓐ.

To save videos & pictures taken in the Notes application in the Photo application, enter the Settings application> Notes, and activate save the photos.

# Scan a document

- In the note, click the Camera button 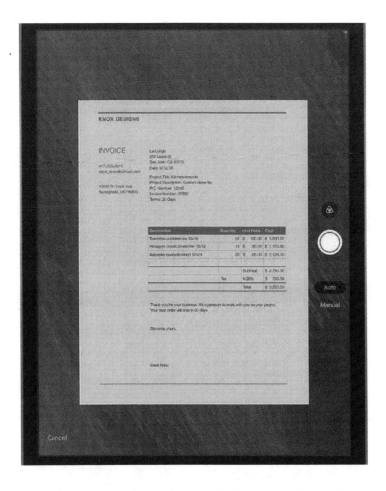, and then scan the file.

- Set the iPad so that the file page appears on the screen; The iPad automatically fetches the page.

  To take the page by hand, click the "Take Picture" button ⭕ or the volume button.

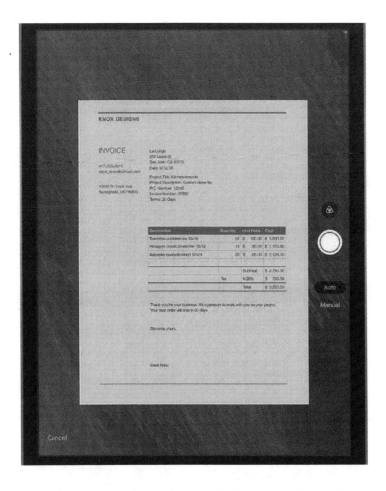

- Scan more pages, and then click Save when done.

---

# Create quick notes anywhere on your device

You can utilize Quick Notes to write information over any application or screen on your device. You can access the Quick Notes in the Notes application.

To create a brief note

1. Do any of the below:

- Swipe up from the lower-right edge of your screen with your Apple Pencil or finger.

- Open the Controls Centre, and click the Quick note button .

  (If you don't see the Quick Note button in the Controls Centre, add it in the Settings application> Control Center, then select Quick Note).

2. Do any of the below:

  - Enter text: Write or type using your Apple Pencil.
  - Add a link: Touch Add Link.
  - Start a new note: Touch .
  - Swipe to go to your other Quick notes.

## To view & organize Quick notes

Click the Quick Notes folder in the Notes application to view your notes.

# Lock notes on iPad

You can set a passcode on your notes to protect sensitive data. Notes makes use of a single login code for locked notes. You can use Touch ID as a possible way to access locked notes; however, do not rely on Touch ID as the only tool to open your notes.

## Setup your note password

- Enter the Settings application> Notes> Password.
- If you have many accounts, pick the account you would like to set the password for.
- Type your password as well as a hint to aid in remembering the password.

  You can also activate Touch ID.

## Lock a note

You cannot lock a note that has PDF, audio, video, Keynote, page, or number documents in it.

---

- Open the note, then touch ⊙ (in the upper right corner).
- Touch Lock.

To remove the lock from a note, Touch ⊙ (in the upper right corner), and touch Remove.

# MAPS

You can view your location on the Map application and zoom in to view the information you want.

In selected cities, Maps provide better information for heights, streets, trees, buildings, architecture, etc.

## Let the maps app use Location services

To look for your location & get correct directions, your device needs to be online & Location Services must be activated. If the Map application shows an alert that Location Services is turned off, click the message, activate in Settings, and then click activate Location Services.

## See your present location

- Click the Track button ◁ .

Your location is marked in the centre of the map.

## Select the appropriate map

The buttons at the upper right part of a map indicate that the map you are in is for driving🚗, exploring🏙, viewing from a satellite🛰 or riding transit🚊. To select another map, adhere to the directives below:

- Click the button at the upper right part of the screen.

- Select another type of map, and then click Close ✕.

## View a map in 3D

Drag 2 fingers up on a 2D map. (When checking out the satellite map, click the 3D button at the upper right of the map.)

On a 3D map, do any of the below:

- Change the angle by dragging 2 fingers down or up.
- View buildings & some other features in 3D by zooming in.
- Go back to the 2D map: click 2D on the top right part of the map.

# USE YOUR IPAD WITH OTHER DEVICES

## Sidecar

With the Sidecar feature, you can expand your Mac's desktop space by using your iPad as a secondary screen. The expanded area allows you to:

- Utilize many applications on different displays.
- Utilize the same application on the two screens.

- Mirror the displays so that your iPad & Mac shows the same thing.

Sidecar requires macOS 10.15 or later.

### Use Sidecar

1. Ensure you are logged in with one Apple ID on your iPad & Mac

2. Use any of the below links:
   - ➢ No wires: Ensure that you have activated the Bluetooth of your Mac & iPad. They must be in Bluetooth range (10m).
   - ➢ USB: Connect your iPad & Mac via USB.
3. On the Mac menu bar, click on the AirPlay menu button , then select your iPad.
4. Do any of the below:
   - ➢ Use the Side car menu on your Mac: You can change the way the iPad works on the Side car menu in the menu bar. For instance, switch between making use of the iPad as a mirror or a separate display, or display or conceal the side bar or TouchBar on the iPad.
   - ➢ Move a window from your Mac to iPad by dragging the window to the edge of your display till the pointer shows up in your iPad. Alternatively, press and hold the pointer above the green button in the upper left part of the window, then select Move to [name of iPad].
   - ➢ Move the window from iPad to Mac by dragging the window to the edge of the display till the pointer is on your Mac. Alternatively, long-press the cursor

over the green button on the upper left part of the window, and select the Move Window back to Mac.

➤ Utilize the sidebar on your iPad: With your finger or the Apple Pencil, tap the icon on the sidebar to display or conceal the menu bar⌴, dock⌴, or keyboard⌴. Alternatively, use one or more modifiers like Ctrl⌃ to use keyboard shortcuts.

➤ Use the Apple Pencil on the iPad: tap to choose items like checkboxes, commands, or files.

➤ Use common gestures on the iPad: Use your finger to touch & hold, zoom, scroll, swipe.

➤ Navigate between the iPad home screen & Mac desktop on your iPad: swipe up from the lower part of your display to go to the home screen. If you want to go back to the Mac desktop, click the Sidecar icon ⌴ on the Dock on the iPad.

5. When you want to stop using your iPad, click the Remove icon ⌴ at the bottom of the iPad sidebar.


## Handoff

With the Handoff feature, you can start things on one of your Apple devices and continue it on another Apple device. For instance, you can start replying to an e-mail on the iPad and finish it in the Mail app on your MacBook. You can use Handoff in many Apple applications, such as Contacts, Safari, Calendar, & some third-party applications.

## Getting started

Ensure you do the following:

- Log in with one Apple ID on the two devices.
- Connect your devices to Wi-Fi.
- Your device should be within Bluetooth range (10 meters).
- On your Mac, activate or deactivate Hand off in System Prefs> General, and Bluetooth is activated in System Prefs> Bluetooth.
- On iPad or iPhone, Handoff can be activated and deactivated in the settings application> General> AirPlay and Handoff, and Bluetooth is activated in Settings.
- The operating system must be iOS 10, iPadOS 13, macOS 10.10, watchOS 1.0, or after.

# Handoff from another Apple device to your iPad

- On the right side of the dock, click the Handoff icon to continue working with the application on your iPad.

# Handoff from iPad to other Apple devices

On the other devices, tap the Handoff icon to continue to work in the application.

The Handoff icon of the application you are making use of on your iPad would show in the following areas of the other devices:

- iPhone or iPod Touch: Under the Application Switcher screen.

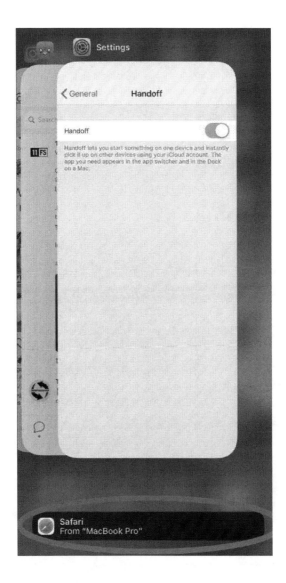

- Mac: The right side of the dock (or the bottom).

## Universal Clipboard

With the Universal Clipboard feature, you can copy or cut a sentence, paragraph, etc. on your iPad and paste it on your other Apple devices and vice versa.

### Getting started

Ensure you do the following:

- Log in with one Apple ID on the two devices.
- Connect your devices to Wi-Fi.
- Your device should be within Bluetooth range (10 meters).

- On your Mac, activate or deactivate Hand off in System Prefs> General, and Bluetooth is activated in System Prefs> Bluetooth.
- On iPad or iPhone, Handoff can be activated and deactivated in the settings application> General> AirPlay and Handoff, and Bluetooth is activated in Settings.
- The operating system must be iOS 10, iPadOS 13, macOS 10.10, watchOS 1.0, or after.

## Copy, cut or paste

Highlight the text, then touch copy or cut, and paste it on your other Apple device.

Note: you must cut, copy & paste the contents as quickly as possible.

# Synchronize your iPad with your PC

You can connect your iPad to a Windows PC or Mac to synchronize the below:

- Audiobooks, songs, books, movies, podcasts, TV shows, playlists, and Albums
- Pictures & videos
- Calendar & Contacts

When you synchronize your devices, you can update these items between your computer and iPad.

Note: If you use other services, such as iCloud or Apple Music, you may not have the ability to sync with your computer.

## Setup Syncing between your Mac & iPad

1. Use a cable to connect your iPad & computer.
2. In the Mac's Finder side bar, choose your iPad. MacOS 10.15 or after is required.
3. Click the type of content you want to synchronize at the upper part of the window (for instance, Movie or Book).
4. Choose "Sync (type of content) onto (name of the device)."
   As a rule, all contents of the internal format are synchronized, but you can synchronize specific items like music, movies, books, or calendars.

5. Repeat the 3rd & 4<sup>th</sup> steps for every content you plan to sync and click the **Apply** button.

Anytime you connect your iPad to your Mac it would sync.

To view or edit Sync settings, choose your iPad in the Finder side bar and select from the options at the upper part of the window.

Click Eject in the Finder side bar before you disconnect your iPad from your Mac.

## Sync your iPad & Windows PC

1. Install or update iTunes on your computer.
2. Connect your iPad and computer using a cable.
3. In the iTunes application on your PC, tap the iPad button on the top left part of the iTunes window.
4. Choose the type of content you want to synchronize (e.g. Movie or Book) in the side bar on the left side.
5. Choose Sync to activate syncing for the type of item.
6. Repeat the 3rd & 4<sup>th</sup> steps for every content you plan to sync and click the **Apply** button.

# Transfer between your Mac & iPad

- Connect the iPad and Mac with a USB
- In the Mac's Finder side bar, choose your iPad. MacOS 10.15 or after is required
- At the upper part of the Finder window, tap on Files, and then do any of the below:
  - ➤ Transfer from Mac to iPad by dragging a file or a file selection onto an application name in the list.
  - ➤ Transfer from iPad to Mac by clicking on the disclosure triangle next to the application name to find the files on your iPad, then transfer the file y dragging it to a Finder window.

To delete a file on your iPad, select it under the name of the application, press the Command-Delete button, and then click the Delete button.

# Transfer files between iPad & Windows PC

- Install or update iTunes on your computer.
- Connect your device & PC with a USB.
- In iTunes on your computer, tap the iPad button at the upper left side of the iTunes window.

- Tap on File sharing, choose an application from the list, and do any of the below:
  - ➢ Move files from your iPad to your PC: select the file you plan on transferring in the list on the right, tap on the **Save to** button, and choose where you plan on saving the file, and then click the Save To button.
  - ➢ Transfer a file from your PC to the iPad: Tap on the Add button, choose the file you plan on transferring, and then tap on the Add button.

To delete a file on your iPad, select the file, click the "Delete" button, and then click the "Delete" button.

File transfers appear immediately. To view what's transferred to the iPad, go to **My iPad** in the Files application on your iPad.

# SECURITY

## Touch ID on iPad

With the Touch ID feature, you can safely unlock your device, allow purchases & payments, and log in to a lot of applications by simply pressing the top button with your finger or thumb.

### Activate Touch ID

- If you did not activate fingerprint recognition while setting up your device, enter the Setting application> Touch ID and Passcode.
- Activate any of the options, then adhere to the directives on your screen.

### Adding a fingerprint

You can add more fingerprints.

- Enter the Setting application> Touch ID and passcode.
- Touch Add a fingerprint.
- Adhere to the directives on your display.

## Label or delete fingerprints

- Enter the Settings application> Touch ID and passcode.
- Click the fingerprint, then enter a name or click the Delete Fingerprint button.

## Deactivate Touch ID

Enter the Settings application> Touch ID and Passcode, then deactivate one or more options.

# Passcode on iPad

For better security, create a code that you must enter to unlock your device when you switch it on or wake it.

## Create or change the passcode

- Enter the settings application, then click Touch ID and passcode
- Click on Change Passcode or Turn on Passcode. To see Options for setting up a password, click Passcode Options.

## Change when your device locks automatically

- Enter the Settings application> Display and Brightness > Autolock, then adjust the timing.

## Delete data after 10 failed codes

Set your device to delete all info, personal, & media settings 10 failed passcode attempts.

- Enter the settings application, then click Touch ID and passcode
- Activate Erase data.

Once the data is deleted, you need to restore it from your backup, or setup the device from scratch.

## Deactivate the passcode

- Enter the settings application, then click on Touch ID and passcode
- Click on Turn off Passcode.

# UPDATE YOUR IPADOS

Your settings & data will not change when you update to the latest version of your iPad.

## Automatically update your iPad

If you did not activate automatic updates when setting up your iPad, do this:

- Enter the Settings application> General> Software Updates> Automatic Update.
- Activate Download the iPadOS update and install iPadOS update.

When there is an update, your device would download the update overnight when it's charging & connected to Wi-Fi. You will get an alert before any update is installed.

## Manually update your device

You can check for & install updates whenever you want.

- Enter the Settings application> General, touch Software.

  You would see the present version of iPadOS that is installed on your device and if there is an available update.

  To deactivate Automatic Updates, enter the Settings application> General> Software Updates> Automatic Update.

## Updates with a computer

- Use a cable to connect your iPad to your PC.
- Do any of the below:
  - ➢ In your Mac's Finder side bar: choose your iPad and click on General at the upper part of the window. MacOS 10.15 or later is required
  - ➢ In the iTunes application on your Windows computer: click the iPad button close to the upper left part of the iTunes window, and tap on Summary.
  - ➢ Tap on Check for Update.
  - ➢ To install any update available, tap on Update.

# SCREEN TIME

With the Screen Time feature, you can control your application usage, set time away from your iPad, etc. You can edit or deactivate any of these settings when you want.

## Set time to stay away from your device

You can block applications & notifications for some time when you need time away from your iPad. For instance, you can set up downtime when it's time to eat or sleep.

- Enter the settings application> Screen Time & activate Screen Time, if you have not.
- Click Downtime, then activate Downtime.
- Choose daily or Customize days, then choose beginning & end times.

## Activate downtime on demand

When Down time is active, only applications, messages, & calls you decide to allow are available. You can get calls from people you choose to **Allow communications with during down time**, and you can utilize applications you have decided to **allow at all times**.

After activating Downtime on demand, a 5-minute reminder would be sent before downtime is enabled. It would remain active till the end of that day or the time your set.

- Enter the settings application> Screen time and activate Screen time.
- Touch Downtime, and activate Downtime till Tomorrow, or activate Downtime till Schedule (if Schedule is activated).
To deactivate Downtime on demand, touch Turn off Down time.

## Set application usage limits

You can set time limits for applications categories (e.g., games or social networks) and for each application in the category.

- Enter the settings application> Screen time & activate screen time if you have not.

- Touch App limit, then click the Add Limit button.
- Choose one or more application categories.

  To set limits for an application, touch the name of the category to view all the applications in that category, and then choose the applications you plan on limiting. If you choose more than one category or application, your time limit will apply to all of them.
- Click Next, then set the time allowed.

  To set a daily time, click on the **Customize Days** button, and set a time limit for certain days.
- Once you have set the limit, click the Add button.

Click the application limit on the Application limit screen to deactivate the application limit for a short time.

To turn off the limit of a category, touch the category, and touch Delete Limit.

## Set communications Limits

On screentime, you can decide to allow or block communications, which includes phone & Face Time calls, & messages from certain contacts in iCloud, for the duration you want.

- If you have not already enabled Contacts in iCloud, enter the settings application > [your name]> iCloud, and activate Contacts.

- Enter the settings application> Screen time and activate ScreenTime if you have not already.

- Click on **Communication Limit**, click on During ScreenTime, and choose any of the below for communication at all times:
  - ➤ Contacts only.
  - ➤ Contact and Group with a minimum of one contact.
  - ➤ Everybody.

- Touch **Back** at the upper left part of your display, and touch During DownTime.

The connection will not go through for someone blocked by your Communication Limits Setting.

## Select the applications and contacts you want to allow always

- Enter the Settings application> Screen Time> Always Allow.

- Under Allowed Applications, click the Add ⊕ or remove ⊖ button beside an application to add or erase them from the Allow application list.
- Touch Contacts to pick the contact you want to allow communications with.
- On the upper left part of your display, click Back.

## Set content & privacy restrictions

You can set restrictions on Application Store & iTunes Store purchases by blocking content that is not appropriate.

- Enter the settings application> Screen time and activate Screen time if you have not already.
- Click on Content and Privacy Restrictions, activate Content and Privacy Restrictions and touch options to set content allowance for iTunes & Application Store purchases, application usage, Content rating, etc.
  You can also set a password that would be asked for before the settings can be changed.
- Choose options to set iTunes & Application Store purchases, application usage, content ratings, etc.

# FAMILY SHARING

After setting up the Family Sharing feature, members of the group can share their locations, subscriptions, purchases, etc. without sharing their accounts. You can also setup parental control for kids.

One senior member of the family - the organizer-creates a family sharing group and asks about 5 members of the family to join the group. When family members enter, they gain immediate access to shared content.

## Setup Family Sharing Group

You only have to setup Family Sharing on one device.

- Enter the Settings application> [your name]> Family sharing, and adhere to the directives on your display to setup family sharing.
- Click on a Feature you wish to setup for the group, then adhere to the directives on your display.

  Depending on the selected features, you might be told to setup a subscription. If you decide to share the Application Store, music, movies, TV shows, and book purchases with members of the family, you agree to pay all of the costs they make as part of the Family Group.

  You can view what you are sharing with your family, and you can customize your sharing settings whenever you want. The features you are sharing with your family are displayed above the ones you don't share.

You can share or setup the following:

- Apple & Application Store subscriptions.
- Purchases: you can share your Apple TV, Apple Books App Store, & iTunes Store purchases.
- Location
- Apple Cash & Apple Card
- Parental Control: You can control your child's purchases and how they utilize their devices.

## Add family members with Apple ID .

Family Sharing organizer can add people to the group.

- Enter the Settings application> [your name]> Family sharing and then touch Add Member.
- Touch **Invite People** and adhere to the directives on your display.

  You can send invitations via Mail, Messages, or AirDrop. If you are close to the person you want to add, simply tap on **Invite in Person,** and tell the person to type his/her Apple ID & login code on your iPad.

# Setup an Apple ID for your child

If the kid is very young to setup their Apple ID, caregivers, parents or guardians can add the child to the Group & setup an Apple ID for them.

- Enter the Settings application> [your name]> Family Sharing.
- Do any of the below:
  - ➤ If you are the Group organizer: touch the Add Member button, click on Create Account for Child, and adhere to the directives on your display.
  - ➤ If you are the guardian or parent: Touch the Add Child button and adhere to the directives on your display.

# Remove someone from the group

The group organizer can remove others. When the organizer removes a member, they are no longer allowed to benefit from any of the features of the group.

- Enter the Settings application> [your name]> Family Sharing.

- Touch [member name], then touch Remove [member name] from Family.

## Leave a Group

- Enter the Settings application> [your name]> Family Sharing.
- Touch [your name] and touch **stop making use of Family Sharing**.

## Disband the family group

The organizer can dissolve the family group. When a group is dissolved, all members no longer have access to the shared subscription & content.

- Enter the Settings application> [your name]> Family Sharing> [your name].
- Touch Stop using Family Sharing.

## Stop sharing purchases with your family members on your iPad

An adult or teen family member may decide that they do not want to share purchase with the rest of the group, they can deactivate Purchase sharing for themselves

- Enter the Settings application> [your name]> Family Sharing.
- Touch Purchase Sharing and deactivate Share Purchases with Family.

  If the group organizer wants to deactivate Purchase sharing, they can click the **Stop Purchase** button.


## Setup Screen Time for a child

When you setup ScreenTime for your kids, you can manage down time settings, application usage allowances, the contacts your children communicate with, ratings for content, etc.

- Enter the Settings application> [your name]> Family share> Screen Time.
- Click on the family member's name, touch Activate Screen Time, and adhere to the directives on your display.

# Activate Ask to buy for your kids

When you setup the **Ask To Buy** feature, the parents, organizer, or guardian would have to approve anything the kids in the group want to purchase.

- Enter the Settings application> [your name]> Family sharing.
- Touch Ask To Buy, and do any of the below:
  - ➢ If you don't have children in your family group: Touch Add Child or Create Child Account, and adhere to the directives on your display.
  - ➢ If you have a child in your family group: Touch the name of the child and activate Ask To Buy.

# MEMOJI

## Create your memoji

You can create your own customized Memoji, and pick skin tones, glasses, etc. You can create more than one Memoji for different moods.

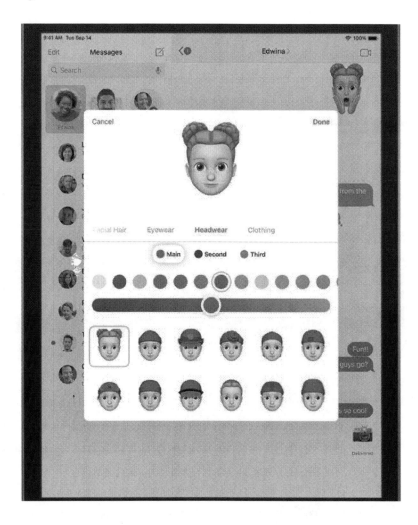

- During a conversation in the Messages application, click the Memoji Stickers button and click the New Memoji button.

- Touch each feature and select the types you want. When you add a feature to the memoji, the character comes to life.

- Touch Done to save the memoji.
  To edit, copy, or delete a memoji, click the "Memoji Stickers" button, click "Memoji", and then click the "More Options" button.

## Send your Memoji and Memoji stickers

The message application creates a sticker bag based on your Memoji and Memoji symbols.

- During a conversation in the Messages application, press the Memoji Stickers button.

- Click a Memoji in the row to see the stickers in the pack.

- To send a sticker, touch the sticker. You can add a note if you wish, click the Send button to send.

# LIVE TEXT & VISUAL LOOKUP

When viewing images in the Photo application , you can utilize the Live Text feature to copy & share text in the picture, translate language, open sites, or call. Images can identify & share details about well-known symbols, art, plants, pets, etc.

## Utilize Live Text

To utilize the Live Text feature, open the image and do any of the below:

- To copy text: Press & hold a word, slide the grab point to get the text you want, and then press the Copy button. To highlight every text in the picture, touch select All.
- Search for text on the internet: Press & hold a word, slide the drag point to select it, and then touch Lookup.
- Translate text: Press & hold a word, drag the grab point to select the text you want, touch Translate.
- Share: Long press a word, drag the points to highlight the text you want, touch **Share**, and choose how you plan to share it.
- Enter a site, call or send an e-mail: Press the text key ⧉, then touch the site, phone number, or e-mail.

## Utilize Visual Look Up

Learn more about the pets, art, famous places, flowers, plants, and more that appear in your pictures (U.S.).

- Open the picture in full screen; The Detected Item Information button 🛈 shows that Visual Look Up info is available for this image.

- Swipe up on the picture or click the Info item button 🛈.

- Touch the icon that shows in the picture or at the upper part of the image information window to see Siri's knowledge and more info about the item.

## Turn on the low power mode

You can extend the battery life of your device through Low Power Mode.

When activated in the **Settings application> Battery** menu, the low power mode would temporarily reduce background activity, such as downloading and receiving emails to extend the battery life of your iPad.

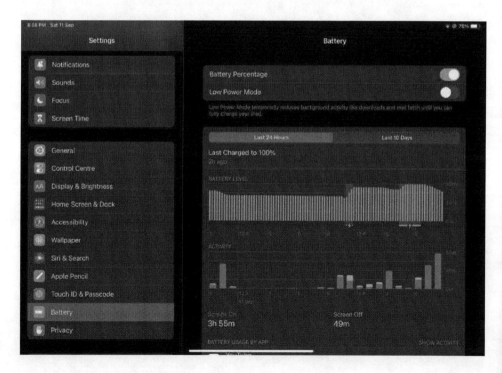

# Use smart lists in Apple reminders

The regular reminders application has received a new addition to Smart Lists. It allows you to setup a Smart List with many conditions for tasks such as Priority, Locations, Flags, etc. Once an added task meets these criteria, it will be added to the Smart list by the OS.

Confused? Let's simplify it for you. You can create a smart list called Birthdays and set a date with #birthday. From now on, when you create a birthday reminder for someone, just add the note to it and it would be added to the Smart List.

# View media information in the Photos application

Apple has finally added an essential info button in the Photos application to view EXIF details of pictures/videos.

The information includes the size of the media, the device that took the picture, its location, etc.

## Keyboard new shortcuts

Apple is offering a global keyboard shortcut for iPadOS 15, which runs across the entire OS.

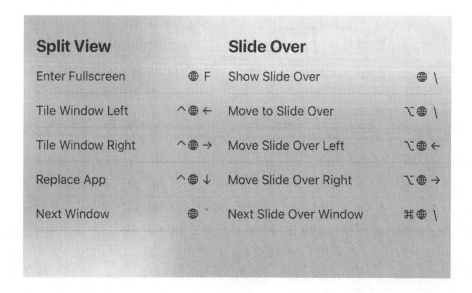

| Split View | | Slide Over | |
|---|---|---|---|
| Enter Fullscreen | 🌐 F | Show Slide Over | 🌐 \ |
| Tile Window Left | ^🌐 ← | Move to Slide Over | ⌥🌐 \ |
| Tile Window Right | ^🌐 → | Move Slide Over Left | ⌥🌐 ← |
| Replace App | ^🌐 ↓ | Move Slide Over Right | ⌥🌐 → |
| Next Window | 🌐 ` | Next Slide Over Window | ⌘🌐 \ |

## System

| | | | |
|---|---|---|---|
| Go to Home Screen | ⊕ H | Siri | ⊕ S |
| Search | ⌘ space | Control Center | ⊕ C |
| Switch App | ⌘ → | | |
| Show Dock | ⊕ A | | |
| Show App Library | ⇧⊕ A | | |
| Quick Note | ⊕ Q | | |

# Write or draw on a picture

- In the Photos application, touch a picture to see it on full screen.

- Touch **Edit**, then touch the Markup button Ⓐ.

- Write & draw in the image using a variety of drawing tools & colours. Click the Add annotation button ⊕ to magnify or add captions, shapes, text, or your signature.

- Touch Done to save it, or touch Cancel if you don't want to save the changes.

Made in the USA
Las Vegas, NV
20 September 2022

55620278R00098